My Book Of Mammals

Written by
Zunairah Rafay
&
Sufia Nasir

Watch this book come to life
in the **lambkinz** app
where books come to life

Download now on

or watch exclusively on
watch.lambkinz.pk

Do you know what
Mammals are?

Mammals are
warm-blooded animals.

They have lots of
hair (fur) on their body.

Female Mammals can give birth and feed their babies.

Did you know humans are Mammals too?

There are more than

5400

species of Mammals on Earth

Many Mammals are at the risk of becoming extinct. This means, they won't live on Earth for long.

We must learn more about Mammals so we can protect them.

Mammals can be

Carnivores

Herbivores

Omnivores

Carnivores are mammals that eat meat. This helps them become strong and healthy.

Carnivores are strong, fast and intelligent because they have to hunt to eat.

They also have sharp teeth and claws for capturing their prey

Lions

Bears

Cheetahs

Wolves

are some examples of Carnivores

Herbivores are mammals that only eat plants.

Herbivores have a set of sharp, blunt teeth. This helps them pull plants out of the ground and chew them.

The most common types of Herbivores are

Cows

Camels

beavers

donkeys

The largest **Herbivore** on planet Earth is

The African Elephant

Omnivores are Mammals that eat both meat and vegetables.

Human beings are Omnivores.

We can enjoy both a steak and a vegetable salad.

There are a high number of **Omnivores** in the animal kingdom.

The most common examples of Omnivores are

Chipmunks

Squirrels

Rats

What's special about Omnivores is that they are flexible eaters.

This makes it easier for them to survive.

Together, we can protect all kinds of **Mammals.**

We can donate extra meat to shelters that house Carnivores.

So, no food is wasted

We can plant more trees to create food supply for Herbivores.

A greater number of trees and growth in greenery will also help our environment.

It is essential to protect all animals from cruelty and help them live healthy lives.

In the end, it is also important to take care of ourselves, as we are Mammals too!

Explore more titles

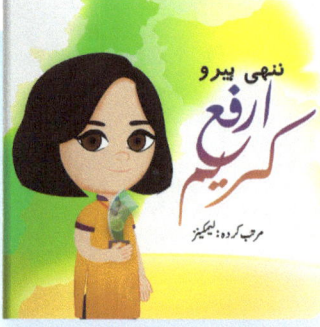

ننھی پیرو
ارفع کریم
مرتب کردہ: لیکینز

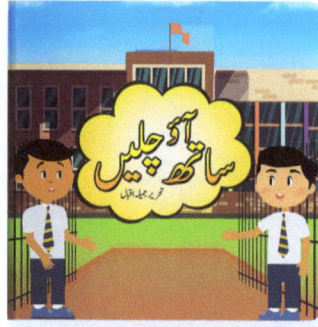

آؤ ساتھ چلیں
تحریر جمعہ اول

حضرت یوسف
اور بادشاہ کا خواب
مرتب کردہ: لیکینز

حضرت یونس
اور مچھلی

پیاری باتیں
دو اہم الفاظ
تحریر
ناصر حسین

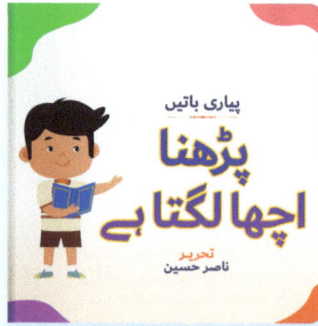

پیاری باتیں
پڑھنا اچھا لگتا ہے
تحریر
ناصر حسین

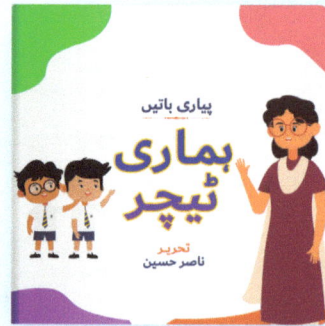

پیاری باتیں
ہماری ٹیچر
تحریر ناصر حسین

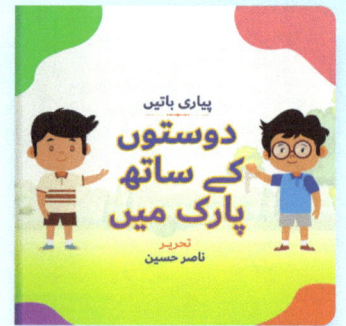

پیاری باتیں
دوستوں کے ساتھ پارک میں
تحریر
ناصر حسین

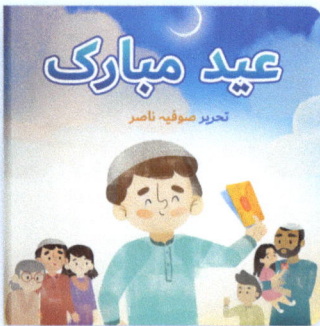

عید مبارک
تحریر صوفیہ ناصر

بقر عید مبارک
تحریر صوفیہ ناصر

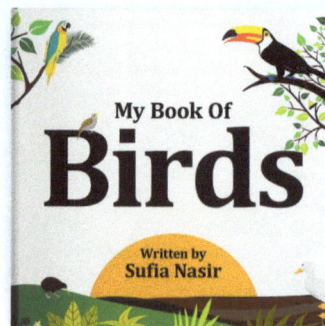

My Book Of
Birds
Written by
Sufia Nasir

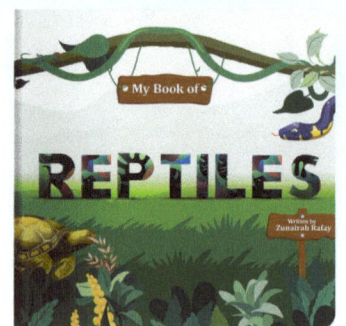

My Book of
REPTILES
Written by
Zunairah Rafay

Watch all our books come to life with playful animation, gentle music & lifelike sound effects in the lambkinz app

lambkinz
where books come to life

lambkinz combines the joy of reading storybooks with playful animation. lambkinz features dozens of gorgeous original stories, general knowledge & instructionals for kids to enjoy & learn from.

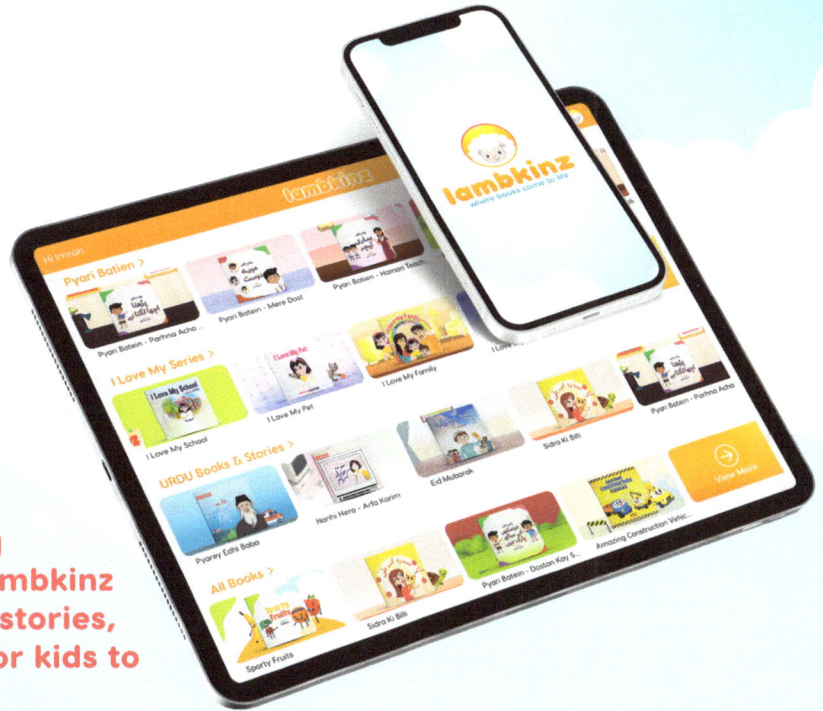

Download the **lambkinz** app for your device.

Download on the **App Store**

GET IT ON **Google Play**

lambkinz is a registered trademark of Green Animation Studio